Date: 7/3/18

**J 966.9 CAN
Cantor, Rachel Anne,
Nigeria /**

by Rachel Anne Cantor

Consultant: Marjorie Faulstich Orellana, PhD
Professor of Urban Schooling
University of California, Los Angeles

BEARPORT
PUBLISHING

New York, New York

Credits

Cover, © Lingbeek/iStock and drbimages/iStock; TOC, © Sabena Jane Blackbird/Alamy; 4, © Bartel Alex/Prisma/AGE Fotostock; 5T, © Novarc Images/Alamy; 5B, © ariyo olasunkanmi/ Shutterstock; 7, © peeterv/iStock; 8, © Lingbeek/iStock; 9, © peeterv/iStock; 10T, © INTERFOTO/ Alamy; 10B, © alarico/Shutterstock; 11, © Eye Ubiquitous/AGE Fotostock; 12, © 1001slide/iStock and © Phatthanit/Shutterstock; 13T, © Olga Miltsova/Shutterstock; 13B, © Danita Delimont/ Alamy; 14, © Peter Horree/Alamy; 15, © Dirk Bakker/Bridgeman Images; 16T, © Michael Graham- Stewart/Bridgeman Images; 16B, © Morphart Creation/Shutterstock; 17, © Frances Roberts/ Alamy; 18, © Richard J Greenman/Alamy; 19, © Gilbertson/ZUMA Press/Newscom; 20, © Fanfo/ Shutterstock; 21T, © Aleksander Tomic/Alamy; 21B, © Banprik/Shutterstock; 22L, © Sunday Alamba/ AP Images; 22–23, © Akintunde Akinleye/Reuters; 24, © Xinhua/Alamy; 25, © frans lemmens/Alamy; 26, © Friedrich Stark/Alamy; 27, © Sunday Alamba/AP Images; 28–29, © Akintunde Akinleye/Reuters; 29R, © dpa picture alliance/Alamy; 30T, © Siempreverde22/Dreamstime, © ET1972/Shutterstock, and © Sementer/Shutterstock; 30B, © aluxum/iStock; 31 (T to B), © Dirk Bakker/Bridgeman Images, © sombo sombo/Alamy, © Frances Roberts/Alamy, and © Akintunde Akinleye/Reuters; 32, © YANGCHAO/Shutterstock.

Publisher: Kenn Goin
Senior Editor: Joyce Tavolacci
Creative Director: Spencer Brinker
Design: Debrah Kaiser
Photo Researcher: Thomas Persano

Library of Congress Cataloging-in-Publication Data

Names: Cantor, Rachel Anne, author.
Title: Nigeria / by Rachel Anne Cantor.
Description: New York : Bearport Publishing Company, Inc., 2018. | Series:
    Countries we come from | Includes bibliographical references and index.
Identifiers: LCCN 2017034341 (print) | LCCN 2017035256 (ebook) |
ISBN 9781684025275 (ebook) | ISBN 9781684024698 (library)
Subjects: LCSH: Nigeria—Juvenile literature.
Classification: LCC DT515.22 (ebook) | LCC DT515.22 .C36 2018 (print) |
DDC 966.9—dc23
LC record available at https://lccn.loc.gov/2017034341

For more information, write to Bearport Publishing Company, Inc., 45 West 21st Street, Suite 3B, New York, New York 10010. Printed in the United States of America.

10 9 8 7 6 5 4 3 2 1

Contents

WARM

Busy

Full of Life

Nigeria is a country in western Africa.

More than 190 million people live there.

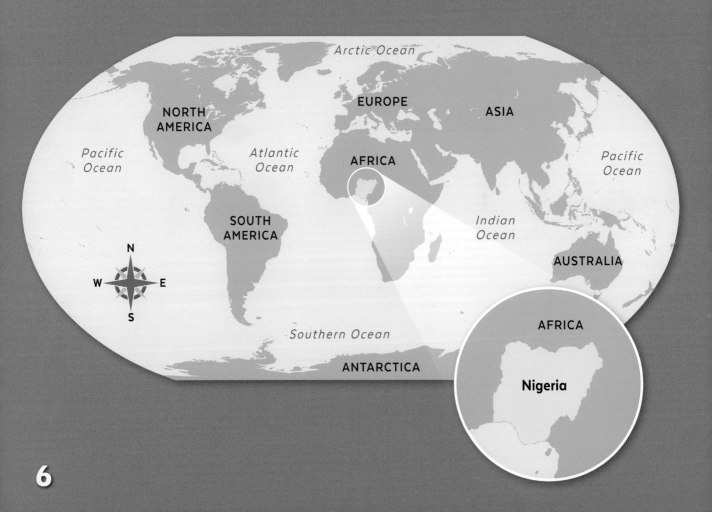

Nigeria has more people than any other African country!

The **capital** of Nigeria is Abuja.

a place of worship in Abuja

However, Lagos is the country's largest city.

Lagos is the biggest city in all of Africa!

More than 21 million people live in Lagos.

Some areas of Nigeria have dense forests.

In other places, there are flat plains.

Rivers twist and turn through the land.

Zuma Rock is a huge rock that's shaped like a dome. It's near Abuja.

11

Amazing wild animals live in Nigeria.

Eagles soar through the sky.

Crocodiles and hippos swim in rivers.

Nigeria is home to more than 1,000 types of butterflies!

People have lived in Nigeria for thousands of years.

The Nok people settled there about 2,000 years ago.

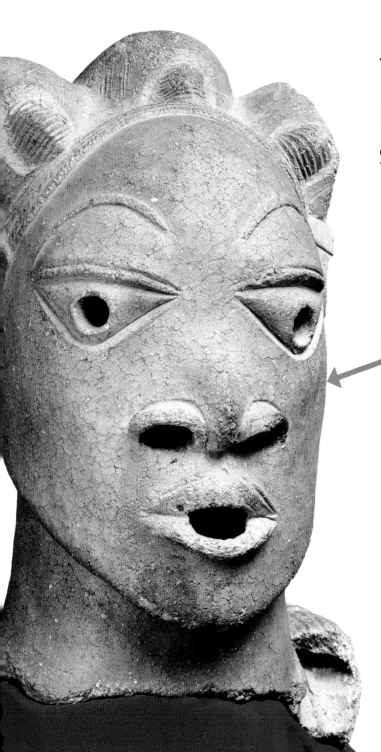

They made beautiful clay sculptures.

Nok clay sculpture

The Nok people also made iron tools. They were among the first groups in the world to do so!

Long ago, African kings ruled Nigeria.

Then, in the late 1800s, England took control.

In 1960, Nigeria became an **independent** country.

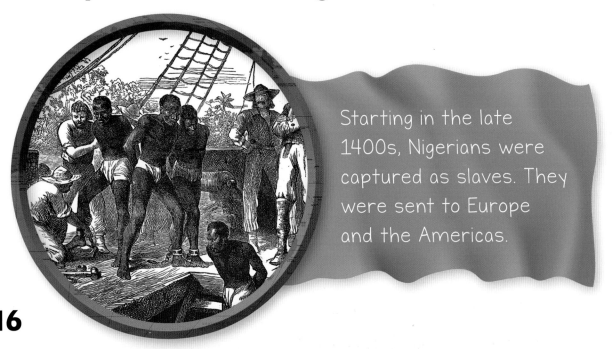

Starting in the late 1400s, Nigerians were captured as slaves. They were sent to Europe and the Americas.

Every year on October 1, Nigerians celebrate their freedom.

17

English is Nigeria's main language.

Other languages such as Hausa (HOW-sah) and Igbo (EE-boh) are spoken, too.

This is how you say *hello* in Hausa:

Sannu (sah-NOO)

This is how you say *hello* in Igbo:

Kedu
(kay-DOO)

Many different groups of people live in Nigeria. Together, they speak more than 500 languages!

Nigerian food is delicious!

Ogbono soup is thick and spicy.

It's made from the seeds of ogbono, a mango-like fruit.

Shuku-shuku are sweet coconut balls.

Zobo is a drink made from red flowers.

There are many festivals in Nigeria.

During the Eyo festival in Lagos, men dress in long white robes.

They dance to honor their **ancestors**.

akete

An Eyo dancer wears a hat called an *akete*.

Fashion is important to many Nigerians.

Some women wear a folded head wrap, or *gele* (GEH-leh).

Geles are often very colorful!

Ankara is a type of fabric with bright, bold designs. It's worn throughout Nigeria.

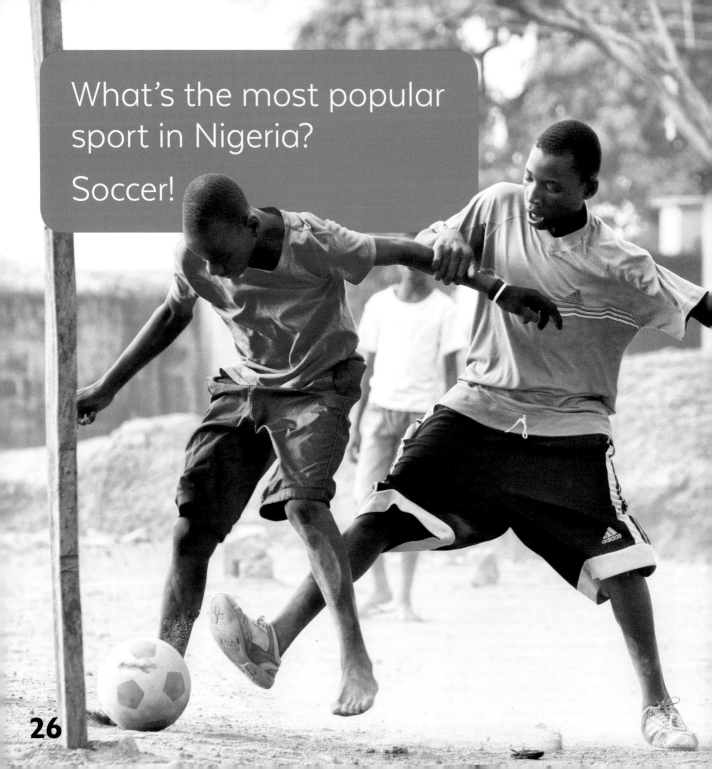

What's the most popular sport in Nigeria?

Soccer!

Other sports are popular, too.

The Hausa people are known for *dambe* (DAHM-bey).

It's a type of boxing.

Dambe boxers fight with one fist wrapped in cloth or rope.

Nigeria has a huge movie **industry**.

It's called Nollywood.

Around 1,000 movies are made in Nigeria each year!

Genevieve Nnaji is a famous Nollywood actress. She has starred in more than 75 movies!

Fast Facts

Capital city: Abuja

Population of Nigeria: More than 190 million

Main languages: English, Hausa, Igbo, Yoruba, and Fulani

Money: Naira

Major religions: Islam and Christianity

Neighboring countries: Cameroon, Chad, Niger, and Benin

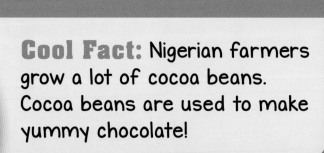

Cool Fact: Nigerian farmers grow a lot of cocoa beans. Cocoa beans are used to make yummy chocolate!

ancestors (AN-sess-turz) relatives who lived a long time ago

capital (KAP-uh-tuhl) the city where a country's government is based

independent (in-di-PEN-duhnt) free of control by others

industry (IN-duh-stree) a kind of business that includes many different companies

31

Index

Read More

Onyefulu, Ifeoma. *Ikenna Goes to Nigeria.* London: Frances Lincoln (2007).

Thoennes, Kristin. *Nigeria (Countries of the World).* Minneapolis, MN: Capstone (2016).

Learn More Online

To learn more about Nigeria, visit
www.bearportpublishing.com/CountriesWeComeFrom

About the Author

Rachel Anne Cantor is a writer who lives in Massachusetts. She enjoys reading books by Nigerian writers, including Chinua Achebe's *Things Fall Apart.*